# Mom



A GIFT

*just for you*

To:

From:

ISBN: 9798716481978

*A mother's love transcends all boundaries even to the point of absurdity.*

*So, here's to all the Moms who love, laugh, and occasionally lose their minds due to the crazy antics of their children. Enjoy these Mom truths.*

Dear Mom,
I get it now...

honestly...
I'm winging it.
motherhood, life,
cleaning, my eyeliner...
Everything!

If I'm missing...
just follow my kids
They can always find
me no matter where
I hide.

I love all the
mythical creatures
in the world...
Werewolves,
Vampires,
Unicorns
Kids who listen.

Sorry, I'm late.
I got into an argument
with my toddler about the
necessity of wearing clothes
in 30 degree weather

My parenting style
has devolved to,
"But did you die?"

# Let them sleep
## for when they wake they
### will move mountains

and shoes, coats, toys, pillows,
more toys, and anything not nailed down

I see those moms
that can do it all
and think...
I should have them
do stuff for me.

My nickname is Mom
but apparently
my full name is

MOM MOM MOM

MOM MOM MOM

Silence is golden...

Unless you have kids
then it is suspicious

Mama Bear is just a euphemism for the fact that I'd tear your head off if you hurt my kids

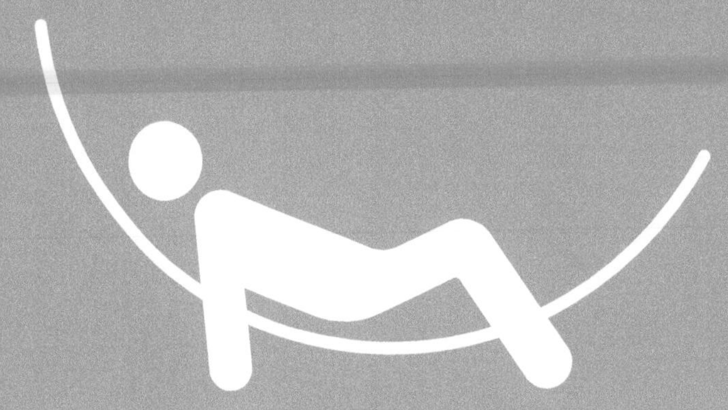

# Hakuna Mytoddler

*It means there ain't no relaxing for the rest of my days*

Based on the amount of
laundry I do each week
I'm sure there are people living
in my house that I haven't met

I adore the parents
teaching their kids
a second language...
while I'm just trying to
teach my kids to put
their pants on the right way

I love how kids can
never seem to find their
shoes, but that speck of onion
in dinner...
yeah, they can find that!

Lean in and whisper
in their ear
It's much scarier...

Motherhood is
an extreme sport
that's why Moms wear
workout clothes 24/7

# <u>Mom Goal</u>

Keep
tiny human
alive

✓ Good job Mom

YOU'RE
THE
BEST
MOM
I LOVE YOU

www.ingramcontent.com/pod-product-compliance
Lightning Source LLC
Chambersburg PA
CBHW042008110726
48006CB00004B/1010